Best Love Poems by Chuan Sha

Best Love Poems by Chuan Sha

Original Chinese by **Chuan Sha**

English Translation by **Chuan Sha** and **Hong Liu**

Bestview Scholars Publishing

Best Love Poems by Chuan Sha

Published in 2022 by
Bestview Scholars Publishing Ltd.
48 Leafield Dr., Unit B., Toronto, ON M1W 2T2 Canada
Email: bestviewscholars@gmail.com
Website: **www.bestviewscholars.com**
Copies of this book may also be ordered from Amazon.com.

Cover design: Alice W. Huang (front cover art by Weijun Wang)

ISBN (paperback): 978-1-896848-24-2
ISBN (epub): 978-1-896848-25-9

Library and Archives Canada Cataloguing in Publication

Title: Best love poems by Chuan Sha / original Chinese by Chuan Sha ; English translation by Chuan Sha & Hong Liu.
Other titles: Poems. Selections. English
Names: Sha, Chuan, author, translator. | Liu, Hong (Translator), translator.
Identifiers: Canadiana (print) 20220411034 | Canadiana (ebook) 20220411131 | ISBN 9781896848242 (softcover) | ISBN 9781896848259 (PDF)
Subjects: LCGFT: Poetry. | LCGFT: Love poetry.
Classification: LCC PS8637.H25 A2 2022 | DDC C895.11—dc23

The author's views and opinions in this book do not necessarily represent those of the publisher.

CONTENTS

Dreams within a Dream

Midnight, I can't fall asleep

The fire begins to die

Wildcats outside begin to yowl as if they have heard

The rats running in the attic

The dust-covered clock ticks along tirelessly

While the spirits wander in the hills, the trees, and the wind.

The darkness rushes in

Through my open door

The sand from my dream begins to flow

The crystal shoes tiptoe lightly

And run above the underflow of the river

Through the shade of the trees

And across the new crescent moon

The shoes walk leisurely

On the windowsill

On top of the broken wall

The roof and the tower

The buds, grass blades, and the moss

Clung with dangling dewdrops
That sigh and moan glimmering
In the night
The surreal neon lights
Unveil the curtain of wish and thought
And weave into dreams
So light
So unreal
So distant in mist
That I feel my exhausted self-shrouded
And put into a deep slumber

You flow to me from the void of my dream
And from the sorrowful solitude
In a sad cloak
Light-footed as a fairy
On the floating clouds
You slowly walk over the spring water
On the journey of love, night dew dripping from your cloak
To my small dwelling
You softly open the net of my dream
Murmuring and mumbling

You bend down and hold my head
With your pretty, soft hands
Your long hair falling upon my face
Tickling my being and intoxicating my

Heart with your fragrance
Your eyes of love have the reflection
Of the night
You cannot help smiling at my
Clumsy poses in sleep
Your teeth are so purely white
Your face beams with happiness
And your eyes filled with the joy of this secret meeting

Softly you shake my head
And shake me into a deeper slumber
Your delicate fingers comb my hair
As if to put your hope
Into my head
Your wide-open eyes gaze
At my peaceful face
As if to see through my eyelids
Into the world of my dreams
The remote and hidden thoughts
That may gallop wildly
Over the impassable trenches
That lead to the inner castle
And the books that cannot be blasphemed
—notes and symbols that belong to me

You bend down to me
Hair falling to cover my face

Your lips on mine, your kisses are wild

Connecting two as one, inseparable

You wander in my dream

As I do

The dust-covered clock still ticks in the still of the night

Bats fly around

Carrying an evil plan in the hunch of their backs

Their wings stir up a cold wind like one from a death valley

Their shrill echoing in a cave

They plan to damage the dream within dreams

A warm corner in this wild cold world

They land on the curtain of the dream

Tearing it open with their claws

To see what is inside

Yet knowing not that most of the dream

Is woven with pain and despair

When the first ray of dawn enters the window

You startle from your dream

With sighs that linger for a while

In my heart

With a bamboo basket

You leave, on the clouds of my dream

Through the flowing sand

Your clothes wet with night dew

There is then no sound as if

Nothing has ever happened

Not a dream in the daylight
Not a single trace of my dream

I awake from dreams of the dream
Then from the dream
Exhausted, eyes blurred
The curtain amidst the mist
The flowing sand glimmering in my dream
The night dew glistening under the stars
The shrill of the bats echoing in the deep
Death valley of my dream
All is gone
Out of illusion
Up to nothingness

I awake from dreams of the dream
Then from the dream
Where your long hair is drenched with fragrance
Where you murmur while holding my head and
Pressing your soft lips
Upon mine
Tears have wetted my pillow
Yet I cannot tell if the water
Is from the pail I got from your well
Or from the basket you took from my garden
Which still has some flowers in it

With buds that squeeze juice from

Shaking

Stems

The Voice

1

Oh! You don't know the voice

You don't know, Mozart

You really

Really

Don't know the voice

It is not "the experience of true meaning"

Nor "the holy music, unsentimental but rational"

Nor that "all that is acceptable will be accepted at will by
receivers"

Nor that "the sound of music is separable"

And it is certainly not "the sound of self"

But it is a voice

A truly "unspeakable mystery" in all existing music

A true "harmony" in all conflicts, which combine

Her "only infinity" and mine

A man and a woman

Two shining stars darting across the sky

Whose bodies glide along the trail

That binds their souls

Into a beam of light

Harmony

Up and down

The hemispheres

Out of the dark western sky in a silvery curve

That rolls and glides and burns to be a

Newborn

Being

She gives birth, screaming like a beast

Her voice boiling the water on the sea

Oh! You don't know the voice

You don't know, Mozart

You really

Really

Don't know the voice

It is the sound

Heard in the depths of night

It is strange to you

But it brings in a new, tender voice

Daybreak follows

From the eastern horizon, unchanged, unchangeable

Since the beginning of time

Filling every

Single day

With magnificence

2

The moon hangs in the sky
We lie on the earth
The night opens its eyes
To marvel at these two naked bodies bathed in moonlight
The sky and the earth
Are visible
And invisible
Like what we are tonight
She is me
And I am her
Fully rounded
Into the moonlight
Ancient and solid, we bear the light
As the Adam and Eve of today
From history's dark end

The sun
Is God Who has created us
To be another being
The bodies of Adam and Eve burn, entwined into a solid
ball: the sun
Then they combine to be a moon
And the moon produces a sun every day

3

Tenderly she said, kiss

Softer

In the dark night

Kiss

Kiss

Kiss...

Oh! You don't know the voice

You don't know, Mozart

You really

Really

Don't know the voice

But I've heard the voice

And I've heard the sound

And I've begun to know

How Adam

Has changed into

Apollo

Kyrie eleison

Kyrie eleison

Kyrie eleison

Christe eleison

Christe eleison

Christe eleison

Sanctus, Sanctus

Sanctus

Dominus Deus

Sabaoth

Pleni sunt caeli

Et terra

Gloria tua

Hosanna in excelsis

4

My dear Lord

If you were born as a human

Tonight, I'd be filled

With your holy

Images

With your honor and with your blessings

Amen

Deep Sleep

You've fallen into a
deep sleep
I look at you
and kiss you, yet
am I in a dream

Ivory lines float over
your beautiful body
your loose hair pours like a waterfall
down till it joins with the white suns.
Your eyes are closed, your lashes long and beautiful,
locking your naughty nature in
with your dreams
What a mask of peace
and of charm
Surprised?
Reproaching?
Disappointed?
Fearless?

Your chin tilts upward; your cherry lips mutter
the beautiful hairy flower blooming in
your groin seems to say
death is not in yet
life doesn't have an end
why don't we enjoy this moment
on the doorway between life and death

Here I kiss you
kiss . . .
my dear delicate love
on your closed eyes
your dream gate
Your vacant eyes belong to a stone statue
that has long sunk into the depths of the ocean
looking back from the other end of life
through the fate that stands between the sea
and the sky
and the sound of
snoring

A deep sleep
you are in a deep sleep
and I am terrified
terrified at being separated from the world
I kiss you

I keep kissing you
while my mind flies to heaven
till daybreak when the sun rises

Inside the Dark House with Open Windows

In the dark house
Where he sat
During his boyhood
The first woman touched him
And opened the front window

In the dark house
Where he sat
During his teenage
The second woman touched him
And opened the window behind him

In the dark house
Where he sat
As a young man
The third woman touched him
And opened the window on the left

In the dark house
Where he sat
During his middle age
The fourth woman touched him
And opened the window on the right

In the dark house
Where he sat
During his old age
The fifth woman touched him
And opened the window overhead

Sleeping Daffodils

The sleeping daffodil
dreams peacefully
in the autumn wind
awakening, in someone's dream

The sleeping daffodil
dreams peacefully
in the spring breeze
awakening, in my dream

The sleeping daffodil
dreams peacefully
in a dream of a dreamer
always, in my dream

The Shadowy Crowds

The shadowy crowds
Of differing shapes, in the sunlight, move at will
Shoulder to shoulder, stepping on each other
You step on my foot
I on his and
Then he on yours
This is when you find
No excuse of hatred
Yet you use the shadow, and use
All its weight in stepping
Restrained in silence and in silent curses
Forward go the crowds
To a dark and strange night

The shadowy crowds
Of differing shapes, in the moonlight, move at will
Shoulder to shoulder, chasing each other in love
He holds your fingertips
You hold mine and

I hold his

This is the time you find that

The eyes are useless, but the shadow that

Drives you to love

Free from shyness

And intoxicate you in kisses and embraces

Forward go the crowds

To a sweet but weird dream

The shadowy crowds

Of differing shapes, in the dream, move naked at will

Shoulder to shoulder

We hold the tips of their hearts by the mouth

They hold yours and

You hold ours in turn

This is the time when no one

Wears anything or

Does anything with the shadows

But everyone straightens their spine

With only courage in their head, and

Walks forward

To the bright but weird day

Midland RT[1] Station

The sky train at Midland RT Station is departing
Its gray doors close, locking in
your smile
your long lashes
your lovely face
All is gone
The willow branches
sway in the wind, wither
upon their past greenness
The gray wooded fence
produces a dry, creaking sound that pounds
on the wooded frame of a mirror, on which
a sad gaze is frozen

My love
her face soft and delicate
eyes like roses
kisses my physical self

---

[1]RT: Rapid Transit, part of the subway in Scarborough, Ontario.

Oh, my heart
my eyes
How many more nights of cynical life
will you go through
before you reach out
and kiss the daybreak that we are dying to see
before we see death

The sky train is departing
its gray doors close
You move on your crippled feet
alone and soundless
with my kisses
toward the line of horizon

Autumn Wind from Dye Lake

The autumn wind smells of Dye Lake
oh, Dye Lake of my town
The wind never smells of the deep Atlantic Ocean
but of Dye Lake
Dye Lake has no chilly current as does the Atlantic
no creatures would raise their heads above the water there
pitiably weeping at the moon: walleyes, rock bass
rainbow trout, silver perches, and
flounder . . .

In the wind that smells of Dye Lake
there are no fathomless blue eyes
The flowing fragrance lingers of chrysanthemums
of bamboos, and pines
The mountain brooks meander pleasantly
where silver carp, grass carp
fish and frogs
play and laugh
full of noisy fun

The autumn wind smells of Dye Lake

oh, Dye Lake of my town

The wind then kept blowing

and there you stood by the lake

You looked and smiled

just like Dye Lake in autumn

the mirror-like water

rippling gently

Raindrops hung on the flowers, the grass, and trees

the tears dripped down your cheeks, into the brook, into

the lake

your lips matched the maple leaves

fallen upon the surface

I found my face reflected, rippled in the clear, pure water

found myself lost in the pine bushes of the silent mountain

The autumn wind smells of Dye Lake

oh, Dye Lake

Tonight

beyond the lake

Robert Burns might hear me

crying

The Night Behind You

You ask what I was looking at—
the night behind you

You ask what I was looking at—
the singing bird in the garden behind you

You ask what I was really looking at—
the night and the singing bird in the garden, behind you

You ask what I saw—
you, the very night behind you
You, the singing bird in the garden behind you

Spring Night

Spring night
waves charge, aiming for the sky
and rush towards the window that faces the dark
Your maiden hair looks as if washed by the night
your eyes shiny, your teeth pearly
your red long skirt dances in the wind
I find my eyes unfocused
before the rosy branches that your laughter clings to
beneath the indigo sky where stars hang
on this spring night

Spring night
is the time that
we sing songs
and drink wine
We shower in the open air
listening to the turtledoves cooing in the valley
insects chirruping in the grass, and
fish and shrimps singing in the brooks

They cry happily
when they mate and play: the crabs, turtles
crocodiles, frogs, and salamanders . . .

Why do we need summer
autumn, and winter
which all fly like an arrow
What follows the sprout is the flower, then the fruit
then its death, and back to the sprout
After the sprout is the flower, then the fruit
then its death and back to the sprout again

Spring night
is the time that
we sing songs
and drink wine
We play with
the strings that make
a web of the spring night

The Mountain Ghost Sings

From the field comes the voice of a woman
a song by a mountain ghost
She sings her way out of the hills
her arms open to the dark void
of the night
shining with the purest of her
naked beauty
She hugs the night
embraces the darkest world
a mountain ghost
Human embraces are not like that
There is no mountain ghost in the human world

The mountain ghost sings on
a female voice to meet daybreak
She sings about the land
just before the day dawns
She sings for the people
who walk at night, and

those who she knows well

the farmers, artisans

tramps, or thieves

the most miserable

in the human world

To graves or heaven

they may go

they remain her closest brothers and sisters

Dawn hears her voice

the mountain ghost's song

The night is over

the sun will be in to see

an evil, ugly

mankind

The Sea Watcher

The woman sea watcher
Imagines what is to be seen
When she looks into
The sea

To and from the horizon the sun
Rises and falls
Yet she remains in the past
When the sun rose and fell

The mist, the clouds wrap him up, making him
A statue right in front of her
Clear and crisp
Like iron

On the surface of the sea
Under the sunlight bloom millions of
White fire flowers
Burning over the roaring waves

Across the vastness of blue

Gradually

Deafening

Until it is absorbed

In paper

Mother Was Just as Beautiful

 I was taking a walk in a garden

Along a trail of cobbled lane

Lined by two rails of evergreen trees

When I saw a young woman in a summer skirt

Beautifully shaped

Marble white skin

Taking the little hands of

A big-headed boy who looked at his mother

With love

The boy walked slowly, clumsily

With endearing hesitation in a

Bright day when the sunshine poured down

Upon the fragrant flowers

After the rain butterflies danced around making

The garden Eden-like in peace

Oh, what a time

It was!

It was also in a flowery garden

That a cobbled lane led to before

The evergreen trees nodding with leaves reaching upward

The sun appeared after a summer shower

And shone on the fragrant flowers around which

Butterflies danced

Peaceful just like Eden

That year Mother was just like that

Young and beautiful

Flower

The flower shows off her color
shaking off a fragrance
from a wet green branch
to the wind
and then withers without a sound

The flower gives out light
burning on the tip of a candle
against the night
splendidly
and then dies out without a sound

The flower looks up to a bird
fluttering among the trees in seasonal colors
in the warmth of the land
chirping sweetly in its glory
and then rests in peace, covered by grass leaves without a sound

Evening Star

The evening star
star of my peaceful night
twinkles like Venus, an eye catcher
in the ocean of stars
The ocean above is so far away
yet the fire burns, followed by
millions of stars that dart towards me
a light of feminine fire!
Oh, the star, as clear and pure as crystal
you shine on my remote past
you shine on my remote future
igniting the fire that burns all to ashes which
you hold in your bosom

Night Song

The night song begins to rise
in spring
from the narrow streets
from the eaves of the houses
from the gilt frames of windows
When a canvas painting is split open
she stands there!
Her long, beautiful hair
tumbling like a waterfall
onto her bare back
singing back to
the night song
she follows
the mermaid
into the depths of the sea
singing and singing
on, and
on . . .

The night song rises

in spring

from the night mountains and fields

Following the mountain ghost's steps

she climbs up a plum tree

naked, delicate

amorous, pure

rivaling the moon and the flowers

She wanders as a lovely nude

about the hills

The mountain ghost is frightened of humans

but how can she sing

so wonderfully

a night song

She sings and sings

on, and

on . . .

Mother

Mother!
You live on the other side of the ocean
That flows to the edges we share
Except, Mother
You are on the east
Where thunder booms
And lightning flashes, different
From what they used to be

The sun was setting behind the hills
And smoke swirled from the chimney
You stood by the river
Drying your hands with your apron
Looking far, to call us back
For dinner

Mother!
You tie your wish
To the trail of the sun on which you ride

Throwing your love, a piece of
Golden thread
With which to bind my heart
When night comes
You pray to the moon
To tidy my dreamy, messy hair
With a tender
Silver comb

Mother!
My dearest
With the Pacific Ocean in between
You've had your son's heart
Clinging to you

Bird on the String

The string
The string I play music with
At the beginning of spring
Attracts a flying bird

The gray bird stands
On the string enjoying
The leisurely time

The summer arrives
The birds stand straight on the strings
Enjoying the leisurely time
Birds of different colors

It is autumn the season to see
The birds flap from the strings
Their claws making a sound that
Lingers, echoes off
As the last note

It is the same gray bird
Standing on the treeless cliff
Against the cold of the winter
Holding my bones
With a leisurely tremble
Playing with my strings
In the whistle of the north wind

Unaware

Oh, the rising sun through the clouds
I was thinking of
Watching you in silence
Unaware that your burning light
Would set me
On fire

Oh, the endless peaks of Mt. Sky
I was thinking of
Climbing up at my own pace
Unaware that your layered mountains
Would lead me
Nowhere

Oh, the endless stretch of the desert
I was thinking of
Taking a lonely walk through you
Unaware that the rolling yellow sand
Would bury me

At the north side of the Fort

Oh, the immense body of the blue sea!
I was thinking of
Rowing a boat over you
Unaware that your roaring waves
Would force me to drift
Faraway!

Oh, the golden cup full of wine
I was thinking of
Tasting it
Unaware that the piercing sweet aroma
Would intoxicate me

Oh, quiet, charming lady
I was thinking
Just thinking, of
Gently playing the strings of your heart
Unaware that your unparalleled beauty
Would send me into
The river of love!

The Sea Beyond the Wall

Beyond the wall is the sea
blue
from light and dark
stretching to
the endless sky

Beyond the wall is the sea
above the sea is the sky
above the sky is sunshine
further above is the sun

Beyond the wall is the sea
that is
all

Beyond the wall is the sea
Yet how could you not
see it until this minute

Beyond the wall is the sea
listen
and listen to the waves
crashing on the beach

Requiem

The girl who knows poetry
Built a nest
In my tree
With brown branches and leaves
The root in her heart

In the palace with no name
Three naked boys
Flap their angelic wings
In the refection of the multicolored glass
While pulling your flowery vehicle
With a white silk handkerchief
They blow the golden trumpets
And play the golden harps
And sing children's songs
And flying accompany you

Your nest is built and it
Clings to the curtain

Of my heart so that
It can embrace and kiss you
During the long day
And night

The children and their souls are lonely
In the night
Come back
Return to
My soul and sleep
During this course of life
In the dwelling of my being
The children have many
Toys right beside
My ears
Be good, and sleep
Don't worry about the snow and ice
Or wolves and tigers
Do not disturb your mother from her dream
She will start her journey
Tomorrow
In the misty morning

The Heart

A heart
Two hearts bound together
Is then called "heart"

The fingertips of your heart
Play the strings of my heart
From which flows the tune of love
The hammer of my heart
Beats on the drum of your heart
From which there is rhythm of love

The arrow of your heart
Pierces through the heart of my heart
Then there is blood
The pen of my heart
Dripping blood
Writes stories in the book of your heart

The seeds of your heart

Are sowed in the field of my heart

From which there is rice

The rice from my heart

Is preserved in the pot of your heart

From which there is intoxicating rice wine

Light Mist

Here they come
Showered in the light mist
girls laughing happily
They run out of the misty doors, one by one
perched upon their heads
are little golden snakes that
huddle in groups, hissing
These girls
their eyes emitting flashes like lightning
wear nothing, so as to expose
their purely white bodies
charming, shrouded
in the morning mist
smelling of sunshine
symbolizing the fairies
who gather in groups

On the left is St. Anna Gate
and on the right David Gate

Remote and

beyond

is the waging blue sea that joins with

the end of the sky above

where Jesus Christ stands

clothed in bark

a glorious cross in hand

pointing to the sun

And

there comes

the clear and piercing

resounding of

bells . . .

The Girl and the Sea

1

The blue sea is wide and free
With light waves pushing its surface
Gently patting the shore
Making foam on the beach
And on the rocks
The water ripples forward
To a palm tree where a girl stands
Carrying a message of love
In a soft whisper
Of sounds

2

Your beautiful hair pours down covering
Your pure white body
A string of ringing giggles follows your footprints
Along the beach
The water kisses each of your delicate toes
And your feet

Then kisses your ankles, knees, buttocks

And your full breasts before

Pushing you up with ease

"Oh, I'm going to float!"

You called out, surprised

The water kisses your soft lips

Your pretty face, and

You try to toss up your head

Shaking off the water

Poseidon laughs and

Covers you with a huge wave

The sea pats you on your pretty face

Kisses each strand of your hairs

And has soaked you

Holding you in the water

Yet you dig yourself out

"Oh my ..."

You cry in frightened wonder before

A huge wave carries you to such a height

That your beautiful body is fully exposed

And momentarily you turn to the breast of the sea

As if to hug it, to kiss it

To lock and indulge yourself in the sea's embrace

The waves fall and rise and push you higher

"Oh, I am floating, I am flying!"

You shout in happiness

You swallow a mouthful of water

And in return shed some happy tears
The sea hugs you
Shakes you and lifts your pure white body
A flower of wonder blooming
Upon the surface of the blue water

3
The sea calms its waves
Which softly flow forward
Sending the girl to the shore
You lie on the beach exhausted
Exposed to the sunshine and the breeze
Gulls fly over the sea that
Has become peaceful and silent
Like a lake surface on a spring morning
Yet the wave that pushes ashore
Kisses the shells
Every single grain of crystal-like sand
And each of your toes
The sea guards you while you sleep
Enjoys watching you the
Energetic girl
A sleeping Venus
And the sea imagines that in the morning
And at night it can kiss you, hug you, and have you—
love you during the horrible time
Of the roaring storm

4

The waves reflect the bloody light of the setting sun
The surface covered with millions of golden rays
Glistening, trembling that create desert in purple gold
Part of the background of the sleeping girl
Naked on the soft sand
Like a Venus in sound sleep
Thick is her long smooth hair
And the sunshine
Makes her an angel at rest
Such a wonderful creature
Her chin, nose, mouth
Her Virgin Mary-like hands
Her full white breasts, smooth curves
Her shoulders, waist, legs
Making a solemnly miraculous universe of
Mountains, valley, forests
Wild fields, glaciers, deserts, which
Attract explorers to sink in and travel

5

Poseidon begins to feel the pleasure
And feel the desire to
Stir the waves, huge waves to
Land on the shore where the girl sleeps
To wake her up

To see how courageous she is
The bright setting sun shines over the sea
That begins to roar like lions at the beach
The rugged rocks tremble in excitement
Shout back in resistance
Like warriors defending their king's castle
Crashing to pieces the attacking waves
Which have turned to blooddrops
The thunderous Poseidon uses stronger force
For revenge by pushing
Destructive waves as high as mountains to the shore and rocks
The sea is burning in a wide fire
In the bloody red of the setting sun
With a loud burning sound flames stretch towards the sky
As if intending to burn down all in their way
And to turn over the bottom of the vast sea

6
You awake giggling from a lovely dream
Stretch
Like a kitten
You shake the water off your hair
Keep smiling at the roaring sea
Until dusk when it returns to calm
Misty air flows by
And rises up into the air
Soft waves kiss and caress the sand and rocks

As if apologizing for their rudeness
Poseidon whispers his tender words to the girl
Till the sun sinks into the sea
And the dark begins to creep in
A silver belt begins to tremble
Leading directly
To the moon that connects the water and the sky
From afar echoing rumbles are heard
The roar of Poseidon from the seabed
And echoes from outer space

7
The girl is amazed at the ever-changing temper of the sea
It roars like a lion and erupts like a volcano
It whispers like a lover ready to sing a lullaby
Changing, unpredictable
It is the symbol of poetry, a source of poetry
Oh, Sea, how many poets have written about you
How many warriors have given their lives to you
And how many cowards have been buried in your depths...

Sunset

The sun is setting
At sunset
I feel homesick
The golden rays spread toward the east
the east where the trees
cast their shadows
the east which is the bright part
of the land
The east is
my home
The sun is setting
At sunset
I feel homesick

The sun is setting
At sunset
I feel sad
It sets off rays
the rays of gold, like those that

flash in my mother's eyes
The sunlight will disappear; then
Mother will leave me and
walk into the dark night
The sun is setting
At sunset
I feel sad

A Star at Night

From the height of the dark night
Falls a silver star
To the ground where you stand
Soundless
Full of light
Right beside you

Oh, my quiet beautiful lady
Are you going to
Bend down
To pick it up
And hold it in your bosom
Or are you just going to
Walk away from it?

From the height of the dark night
Falls a silver star
To the ground where you stand

Man and Woman's Primitive Act

The scene of that primitive act
Is of a man and a woman
Kneeling before flowers, in the moonlight
They would see the sun appear from behind the hills
Crashing waves, the valley, the forest
And the eternal stone gate cannot separate them,
Where there are moss, vines, lizards
Centipedes, scarabs, and fireflies...
Under the aged apple tree
Roamed the first couple
Who hummed the first love song
Lovers, afterwards, had their names carved on tombs
Or printed in poems
Or on the fossils of the dead volcanoes of Pompeii and Fuji
Or on the fresco paintings from Mt. Gu-Yin, the Harlong
Valley and the Mogao Grottoes
Or on wax printing cloth beneath the Taklamakan Desert
Sunken ships in the Mediterranean Sea
Stone sculptures in the pharaoh's tombs

And the paintings of lovemaking on the walls
Of the imperial palaces of ancient China and India
All this was written on pages of love

Dew puts her arms around grass's neck
Stamens and pistils lock themselves
In kisses
The fire from trees licks the grass
Making entwined flames gold and silver
The trails of mixed smoke
Reach the garden of Eden where
Adam and Eve touch each other, lost in intoxication
The pink stems and buds are
Singing to future generations
Singing of love
Love
Love . . .

. . .

The scene of that primitive act
Is of a man and a woman
Is it not an eternal secret
And a gravity of the Lord Almighty
That attracts all creatures?

The Wind

The wind whistles past
To the long-gone ages
To the riverside
It sweeps
The green leaves
Of the sugarcane plants
Growing by the beach
It brushes the leaves of February
And blows high the beautiful hair
Of my lady

The wind whistles past
To the long-gone ages
To the riverside, by which
I saw your charming figure
In the spring of February
A green, green life

The wind whistles past

To the long-gone ages
To the
Riverside
I return
My heart vacant
Hands empty
With the wind...
Longing to kiss you again
But where can I find you
My lady?

Holy Light

Holy light
from the past
still the future
Holy glow?

dusk
in the meadow by the forest
in the cloudy sky
the swaying, rolling dark clouds suddenly cracked open
a long beam of light shot into the vast mists
shrouding us

your
beautiful hair, eyebrows, nose
smiling, quivering lips, white teeth
magnolia-like palms, fingertips, and raised skirt corners
all glittering

hiromi
I am alive and bright
leaves are flying
billions of happy grass blades in the green meadow
screaming and singing in the wind
swallows, sparrows, crows, dragonflies, butterflies, scarabs
are dancing wildly
everything is bathed in the
radiance of the Holy Spirit

like
that summer night four years ago
in the forest
the moonlight that cut through the night sky like a silvery
waterfall
adam and eve
covered with no leaves
that fluffy dark-gray little fellow
the awl-like bright and playful gaze in its eyes
squeaky sound between teeth
canada's kobayashi
separated a fiery light

Holy Light
from the past
still the future
Holy glow?

but now
it comes alive
Divine Flash

joyful and full of melancholy
but from the far
past
or future
night sky galaxy
the river flows to the depths of the sky

grasp my heart
happiness
dark clouds overhead
and our hearts
on the rock wall of the sheet
swaying and rolling
anesthetized into
fossils of sighs

Summer Shadows in Winter

in winter

summer shadows

church spire and that thin skirt

rustling summer days

your pouting mouth

whistling

mumbles out

car horns

taut on thighs

black stockings soft melody

pink-note heels

from my palm

step on the clutch

footprints on the beach

floating in the blue lake

in the summer sun

and the scent of your body

lakeside

whilst your skirt swells up with white foam

from that red rock rolls out summer

until it

covers

this black jazz winter

The Third Tree

your heart
often
jumps
inside me
makes me feel
time stand still like a wonderland

from the waning moon floating over the lake
to the full moon hanging on the treetops
the beast sees us like
wild primitives
you let me
Stay away from the dirty clothes of human beasts
and go back to cleanness
how joyful and happy you make me
a beast
a being

from body to soul

the annual cycle has turned six times
in my eyes
behind your eyes
a shadow fades
in between two trees
vaguely
holding your arm

look at
spring, summer, and fall
winter
sees the third tree
tears
turn into drifting wintry snow

Back in the Past

back in the past,
as far back as our innocent childhoods
far far away
as far as Luoshui and then Yunmengpu
very deep
as deep into the sky where we tour together

dream
looking back through the endless autumn waters
unexpectedly
tonight
you appear in front of me
like a meteor flashing across
my starry sky

Spring Girl

Love at first sight
but it is like taking a thousand-year journey
with the bright moon millions of miles apart
meant for each other
another amazing classic date
your voice and face are found only
in the mirror?

A girly slender figure walks in the spring mist
Autumn's swaying waves pierce through my soul
giggling
the shadows of your hands breaking chestnut petals
caress
my bolt of dreams and
my window lattice

The moonlight dances
its long sleeves
hook away my heart

milky way
dawn at Dongyu
bathes your eyebrows
in the red rising sun

I wake up
in fear of falling into the water
a pond of broken lotus leaves

Beautiful Eyes

Why am I ascending?
everything becomes holy
if diamonds are precious
now
I am a diamond sculpture
if the Broadway stage made me a star and put me in spotlight
then
I would rather hide behind you

At this moment
I am right by beside you
your face
your beautiful eyes
dim the entire world

Blue Skirt

The blue skirt
covers the woman, who feels
the passion of the sea
An irresistible, trembling desire is felt
as if it were a pack of hungry wolves
Stares and gazes that are like waves
rush towards the woman's body

The wind begins to moan
and blows up
the skirt
Choked with a deeper, further, and wider thirst
The wolves watch the blue skirt being blown
rustling, into the distance
over the sea

Red Skirt

Oh, my lady in
the red skirt
You are the dream
that haunts the poet
a flower that blooms
in the light
on the stage
You are the first line of lyrics ever written,
the last note ever sung in an opera
You are the water in an autumn lake
at the bottom of which the fish swim
You have seized us all
and seized the light of
the world
You are the water in a brook
clean water that flows
through my cupped fingers
You are a song from the mountain
where birds sing and soar

and trees crane up their heads
to listen
There you are, in the red petals
the white anthers
the black sepals.
Flying overhead
you fall gently
into a dream
into a river that runs through the land
sparkling in the sun
with numerous men's eyes afloat
Oh, my lady
my lady in the red skirt
you are the dream
that haunts the poet

Silver Skirt

The skirt is silver
and the lady is silver
in the silver skirt
In the dark night
she knits
and she hums a childhood song
In the song she finds herself dying
and then reborn
In the singing she is singing and disappearing
and she is happy and sad
Fingertips of the moon
play about as if in a dance
the stars are knitted, one after another
into the sweet dreams of her son
Moonlight flows through her life loom
turning a silver corner of her skirt
into a new coat for him

The skirt is silver

and the lady is silver

in the silver skirt

At dawn

she is waiting

waiting for her son

her golden son

her son of gold—

her Sun.

Green Skirt

Green Skirt
the lady in the green skirt
you are the fields and the forest
abundant and rich
with clusters of fruits hanging from trees
Moonlight flows in after sunset
and sees the love banquet
where you cover your man
cover the land and the forest
The fields are burning
in your promise
In the depths of the night
the fire shoots into the sky
You are the fire of the fire
fire of the land
fire of the rocks and stones
fire under the water, and
the fire that burns inside your man
You a fire spirit

hidden inside
the green skirt

It is autumn when
fruits hang from the trees
and the animals sing in chorus
Oh, lady
in the green skirt
you are green
singing
a green song
joyful, proud, and
intoxicated
in the green
by your own amorous instinct
Rejoicing and worrying
you wonder if the day will come
when the volcano erupts
In front of you there is a silent door
you are outside of it

Black Skirt

Oh, the lady in black
in the black skirt
in the black veil that covers all
but your eyes
eyes like precious stones, reflecting
your thirst
The deep sea
has taken the lives of many men
and buried their chilly white bones
in its fathomless bottom
On the night of the full moon
your tree rises through the surface of the sea
and the bones put on flesh, then clothes, and gather atop
The wild dancer among them is you
Naked without the skirt of the ocean
your body looks all white
as you hold the moon in your mouth

You are Cleopatra of the Nile

whose nose draws the map of history on a coin
You are a siren of the Mediterranean Sea
whose songs lure sailors to their death
You are a goddess of the Aegean Sea
whose stare brings the warriors to their knees under your skirt
You are the priestess of Apollo
whose wisdom turns all men into fools

It is only at night
when your songs are clear and piercing
that the bird flies into your cage
That black and sensual palace of music, your cage
where fine black wine is served
and a black flower
with a lethal fragrance
crawls into
bed
in the dark night
whispering into her lover's ears
while trembling
and fully open
Oh, you sit in front of a mirror
appreciating every move you make
Black Skirt
the lady in the black skirt
in the black veil that covers all
but that pair of eyes

which like precious stones
bring forth the dawn
and the sun that rolls up
from the surface of the sea

Golden Skirt

Oh, the lady in the golden skirt
the lady in gold
the lady of gold
she is the wife of a farmer
a daughter and the daughter of a mother
a daughter and the mother of a mother
the daughter of the river
the mother of ancient times
She is in the mountain
in the river
on the high, high wind
She is in the dream, galloping with her man on a white horse
singing an old folksong

She dreams of her man who had buried her a thousand times
who died long ago
She walks on the fields, where flowers bloom and wither
through the villages where cooking smoke rises
She bathes in the brooks
and litters her way with precious stones

Oh, the lady in the golden skirt
the lady in gold
the lady of gold
she walks from sunrise
to sunset
from dawn
to dusk
She pauses atop the hills
and waves goodbye
to the girl who follows her
saying she alone will walk
through the sea of night

On the other side of the night
stands a lady
in a silver skirt
her mother
who holds a rainbow skirt
waiting for the day
to come
After a bath in the sea of night
she holds to her bosom the cotton clothes
for her baby girl
in mixed colors
the colors of Spring

White Skirt

1

The white skirt

my lady wears

covers her in white

Oh, lady of the day

the sun

and the moon

You are core of the fire

a silver-white fire that seeks the truth of color

Feelings of love

flash in your eyes

female murmurs escape your cherry lips

Your beautiful arms

your holy pure, marble-white face, neck, and full breasts

remind me, my lady, of the amazing chinaware

produced in the Yuan and Qing Dynasties

you remind me of the holy body of Guan Yin[2]

and of a ripe, juicy fruit hanging on a tree

---

[2] Guan Yin: Goddess of Mercy.

Your feminine fire, joined with spectrums
licks the shadows, seductively, from your matured self
and burns inside your soul and virginity
You are the fire
that burns all
your lovers

2

Your lover, my lady
is poetry
is a poet
male poetry
a male poet—a male flower radiating with golden rays
Your lover is the land, the ocean, the sky, the sun, and Man
the man of men and poet in the kingdom of poets
You find him in a statue from the Mediterranean Sea
in fresco paintings of Dunhuang, Mt. Gu-Yin and the
Harlong Valley, in the forests of Georgia, Poland, Hungary
by River Don
a warrior on a golden horse, or a silver one, or a marble one
a Khan of Mongolia who aims his fully drawn bow
at a flying eagle
Oh, my lady, your man gallops
from yesterday to today, to tomorrow
from dusk to dawn
from the edge of the grassland to the edge of the sky
and he ponders

Oh, my lady
your lover is from the thread-bound books
a witness of the chessboard war between Liu Bang and Xiang Yu
at Crane Ditch in the West Han Dynasty
a General Xiang who groans in his concubine's arms
after being defeated in a battle
Oh, my lady
your lover is a Chinese scholar dressed in a long gown with
a silk cap
wandering about in the 21st-century Europe
daydreaming of a horseback fight among skyscrapers

3
The white skirt
my lady wears
covers her in white
Oh, lady of the day
the sun
and the moon
you are the land
the sea
the sky

Indeed, you are
you are the land, the sea, and the sky
you are the green grass in spring
the colorful world of summer

the animals in the deep forests
a two-legged being in the city and countryside
You are everything
that belongs to
the sun
that is under the sun
You are everything
that is under the moon
that makes a man's life
You are a man's moon at night
the soul and spirit
that drag him around at night
when he looks through the mirror at
the unpredictable changes on the screen of the night sky

4
The white skirt
my lady wears
covers her in white
Oh, lady of the day
the sun
and the moon
You are the beauty of the sea
you are the rising moon that plays
with the fragments of the sunset on the sea
you are the setting moon that combs coquettishly
in the mirror of the rising sun

You are fair, charming, and infinitely beautiful
you are a door between the sun and the moon
you turn your back to both and the stars and the eyes
that you face, meet and swallow
You carry on your back a basket,
as empty as your years
that you use to catch the moon floating on the water

Your eyes
are like those of an ancient Roman statue
lost in thoughts
one open and one closed
one in the dark and one in the light
both with tears of happiness and sadness
Oh, your eyes, my lady
when can they become like those of
Venus of ancient Greece, who
tossed her head at the sun
When can they open
with joy and charm

5
The white skirt
my lady wears
covers her in white
Oh, lady of the day
the sun

and the moon

you are a pearl-white beauty

In a summer night, the moonlit fog dampens the fields

at dawn the sound of a song pierces the rosy mist

over the desert, the grassland, the forest

to where the water and the sky meet

over laughter and tears, both bitter and sweet

A naked mountain ghost drags a leopard off the hills

singing all the way

That's all you have become at night, lady

in your man's arms

a dreamy weaving girl

6

The white skirt

my lady wears

covers her in white

Oh, lady of the day

the sun

and the moon

you dream of your lover

The skirt, the flesh, and white whispers

you are Venus

truly

You are a lily

white with splendor

listening in the dark to a poet's song

Trembling, my lady, you find yourself

in the midsummer night

flying, and flying

toward the sky

full of stars

J.J. and the Dream

Is that you, J.J.?
Or am I dreaming?
Who are you?
The stars are shining
Over the window
You smile, clear and pure like water
And walk to me
You sit on the windowsill of
My dark house dangling your feet
While the morning star twinkles
Half of your face lightens up
Though not as bright as the other half
Covered with a curtain, a curtain
Of dark
Or the one by Poppaea
I see you sitting there
As quiet as the night
I can feel your pure soft skin
Like feeling the lake water

On the windowsill of the dark house
There is no time and space except
You and me alone
Somewhere is the dim curved light of the night
You walk toward me naked through chain rings
The tenderness in your eyes draws me to the lake's bottom
Green vines grow from the bed of dreams
To tangle our bodies burning
In the fire of desire
Your beautiful hair is
Soaked in my sweat
Oh, my queen
Do you still remember me
Crowning you beside the lake
Of summer?

In the fields outside the window
Stand rows of scarecrows
Water light is seen faintly shining from afar
Pale gray banners flap in the wind in the graveyard
Right beyond are the lakes connected to the sea
The end of the sea is the continent of East
Where my ancestors shed their blood

Is that you, J.J.?

Or am I dreaming?

Who are you?

The stars are shining

Over the window

You smile, clear and pure like lake water

And walk to me

Oh, my beauty

White threads of smoke are waving in the open field

A dragonfly flaps its glistening wings on a blade of grass

Yet why do you come

Just like a dream

Where you seem to

Wear nothing

In a dark night

Your sunny shadow melts into the blackness

And in a broad day

Your moonlit shadow vanishes into the sun

Is that you, J.J.?

Or am I dreaming?

Who are you?

The stars are shining

Over the window

You smile, clear and pure
Like lake water
And walk to the calling dawn

At Dawn

The day is dawning
A turnstile that separates
Brightness and darkness

The dark night
Holds its breath
Leaving without a sound

There is no sound of footsteps
Nor of undressing
The white crescent alone
In the sky
Smiles at the
Morning star

I can see the days
That have passed
The ferry boat jumped in the waves
Of the grandview river

The window of my heart
Opened in the flowers of your smile
Leading to the splendid views ashore
How beautiful were the flowers in the early spring
Trembling, fresh in the rising sun
How we loved each other
The window was open as we sailed
And closed when the ferry landed ashore

The anchor hit the shore
Its chains making heart-broken sound

The day is dawning
The dark night leaving without a sound
The female animal is alone
Its pubic hair shimmering
And it is as quiet and mysterious as the sky
Oh, my beauty
This is the time
The hour of the dawn
When you are most charming
The hour that you lock me
In your love
The fingers of my eyes
Wantonly play over the keys of your body

The day is dawning

The treetops become rosy in the light

From the end of the lake

The newly painted wooden stairs moan

Under your feet that are leaving

The feet

Delicate and amorous

Covered with my kisses

Shine in the disappearing

Darkness

Acknowledgements

Chuan Sha and Hong Liu thank Freeman J. Wong for donating his precious time to editing their English translation and everybody else who has helped make this publication possible.